Catherine
with best wishes
Richard Holam
3. October 2008.

flowers...

Richard Haslam

This book is one of a special first edition of 1500

For Dodie
Neville, Alison and Caroline
With Love

4

Foreword - JO READ
Flower Council of Holland (UK)

The land of our birth has a profound impact on the emergence of our character and a lasting, if occasionally startling, influence on our individuality and the development of our own style. No matter how much we are tempered by travel, chastened by chaos and enervated or exhausted by experience, our roots show through.

Was it ever thus with Irish folk? Engaging, infuriating, wholehearted, some of the finest drinking companions the world has seen and frequently gloriously creative. It is a glove-like description for Ireland's foremost florist.

Over the last twenty years, Richard Haslam has, in my opinion, been the most influential florist to emerge from the 'Emerald Isle'. His unique take on creativity has inspired the thousands of floral students all over the world who have listened to him and watched him demonstrate.

But it all stems from the Irishman in him. For Richard's boundaries are elastic not fixed, rules are ideas to be interpreted not rigorously followed and the coastline is always excitingly turbulent not cosmetic calm!

Nature inspires him and, curiously, his mind is not dissimilar to the Irish landscape, oscillating from the rocky shores of Galway Bay or the stunning lakes of Killarney to the incomparable drama of Connemara. Just like Ireland, he doesn't do predictable!

As you will see in this remarkable book, despite his fame and his work in Europe, America, Africa and Asia, at heart Richard is still the trained Irish horticulturist that he has always been – albeit with a sizable dose of ever-changing creativity thrown into the mix.

Jo Read

...I love flowers,

I am passionate about flowers,

I work with flowers...

...hardly surprising as I grew up in a family of great gardeners, talented florists and artistic flower arrangers. My childhood immersion in the world of flowers had a strong influence on me, as I embarked on a career in horticulture. This training provided a depth of knowledge and skill which was vital when I progressed to the more creative profession of floristry. I travel all over the world demonstrating the craft and teaching the art of design using plant material and flowers as a medium.

Although I have seen many styles and techniques, my first choice always returns to simplicity; uncontrived displays that focus on the flowers and their exquisite beauty.

It is tempting for one to try too hard and lose respect for the individual flower. In an effort to emphasise the fragile beauty of a flower and highlight its individuality, I sometimes use just one variety in a design or a monochromatic colour scheme.

When I make a wedding bouquet, I very often use only a few flowers. Colour, texture and quantity are used, particularly in church flowers, to create maximum impact in large areas.

Different people draw their inspiration from different places; for me, the colours and textures found in nature are powerful. This influence is never static with the ever changing Irish weather and light. The cameo pictures of Irish landscapes are intended to demonstrate this creative source. Landscapes seep into my being and reemerge as flower designs. Colour and form in architecture, fashion and interior design are the daily experiences of life that inspire unique creations

My sincere hope is that this book will inspire you...

       enjoy!...

Richard Haslam

9

flowers...

landscapes and seascapes...

Living beside the sea, woods and mountains, is a continuous source of inspiration. The ever changing forms and textures seen in branches, leaves, mosses, sand and water create an intriguing backdrop for a new work. There is always something new to complement flowers, giving tremendous scope by juxtaposing the medium against a growing environment, which both, in essence, are changing.

flowers ... in Church...

Throughout history flowers have been used consistently in places of worship. Irish churches are rich in character, allowing for dramatic environments to place floral pieces. St. Nicholas' Collegiate Church, Galway, records that Christopher Columbus visited on his way to the New World in the 15th Century. St. Flannan's Cathedral in Killaloe has examples of Romanesque Architecture, Ogham Stone and an 11th Century High Cross.

Echoes of Early Christian art in ancient churches influence my designs. In turn, these Holy sites complement displays, enhancing the freshness of flowers placed in an atmosphere of evocative time-worn elegance.

flowers... lifestyle and interiors...

Like changing fashion, I continually vary flowers to create innovative designs to reflect new trends in society. Colour, form and fabric inspire my use of fascinating sundries, lush Irish foliage and dramatic flowers to produce spectacular living interior designs. Aghadoe Heights Hotel is the photographic venue here. This is one of my favourite locations, its unique view over the Lakes of Killarney offers a breathtaking contemporary backdrop for these original concepts in lifestyle designs.

34

37

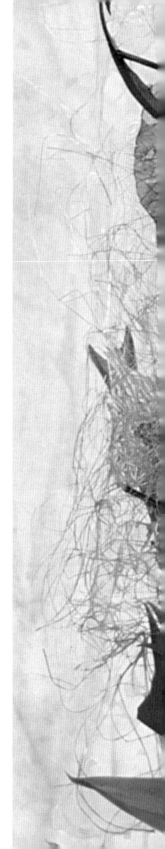

51

flowers...

weddings...

It is such a compliment to be asked to design flowers for one of the most important days in a couple's life. Ambience and drama are created by selecting colours and designs that enhance the choice of dress and venue. Whether flowers are 'en masse', or with individually crafted bouquets, attention is given to creating designs that become memorable 'conversation pieces'.

When guests express their appreciation of the overall effect, it is a measure of the success of my collaboration with the bride and groom.

57

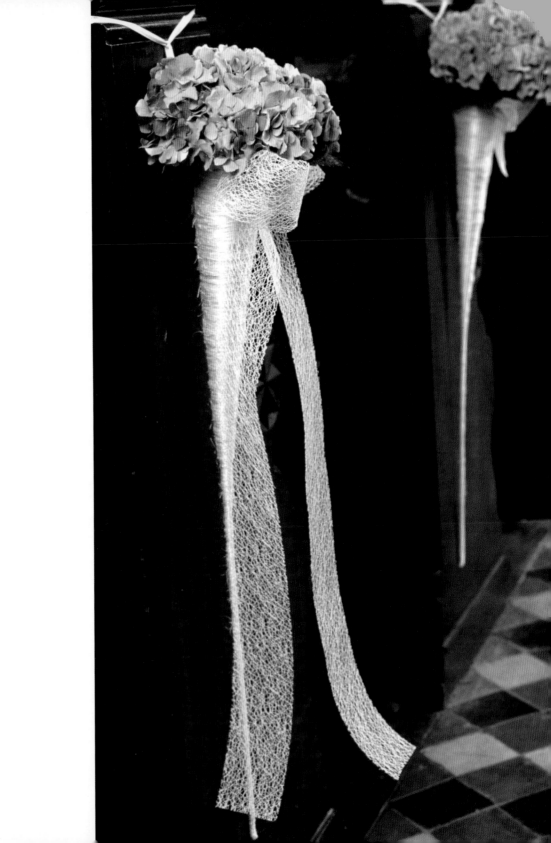

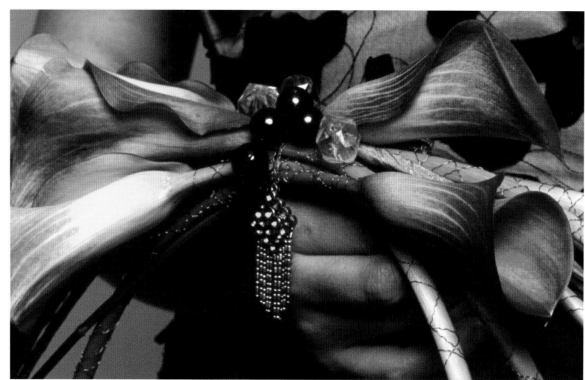

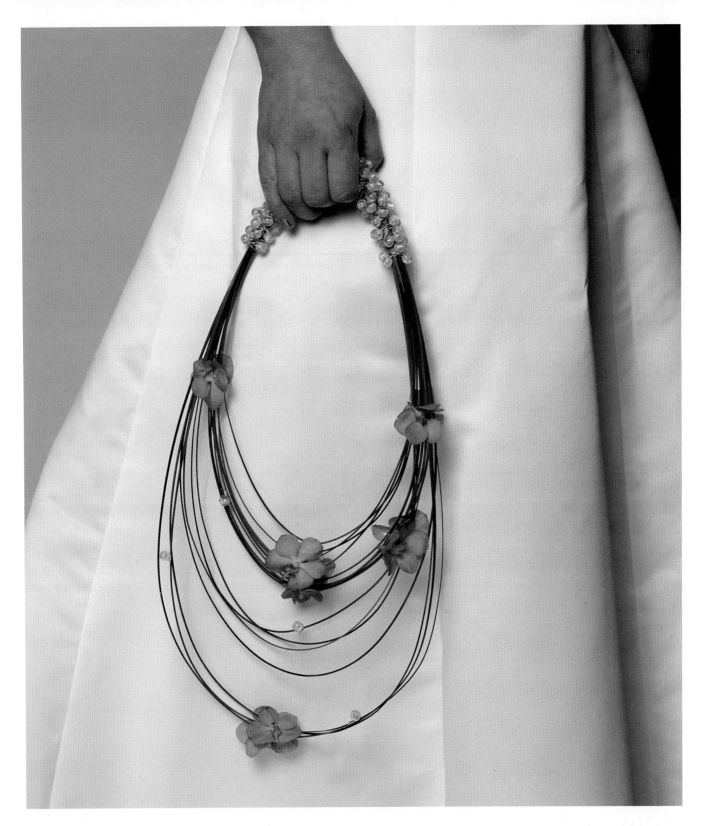

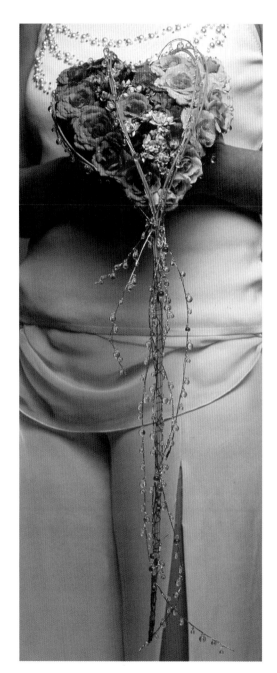

flowers...

seasons and occasions...

Seasons create moods and a sense of perspective in my life. Each one has its own unique importance; buds and f lowers in Spring, the riot of Summer colours, Autumn flowers, berries and leaves, the bare branches of Winter. A calendar is marked out by birthdays, love days, happy days and sad days.

I also enjoy the challenge of recycling materials into artistic sundries; an empty chocolate box, an egg carton and even egg shells. Almost everything has its one last use.

There are flowers and designs to suit every event . It is no effort to work with well chosen materials that suit the season or occasion;
my time clock is in tune with nature.

spring...

v
a
l
e
n
t
i
n
e

m o t h e r s

d a y

e

a

s

t

e

r

summer...

91

autumn...

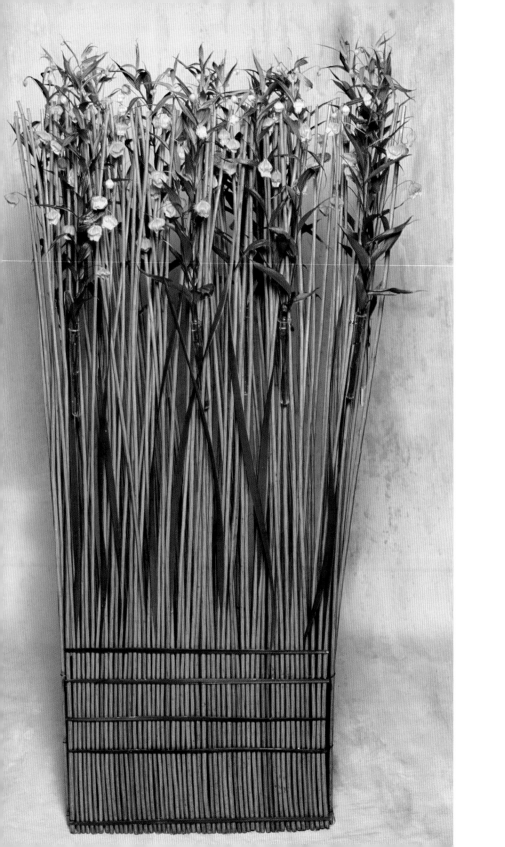

winter...

Christmas

Index

Delphinium Elatum
'Cream Arrow'
Delphinium Elatum ' Alie
Duyvensteyn'
Hydrangea Macrophylla
Delphinium Ajacis
(Larkspur)
Paeony 'Sarah
Bernhardt'

Paeony 'Shirley Temple'
Lily ' Willeke Alberti'
Matthiola Incana (Stock)
Syringa Vulgaris 'Ruhm
Von Horstenstein'
Asparagus Setacues
(Plumosa)
Danae Racemosa (Soft
Ruscus)

Chamelaucium Uncinatum
'Snow Ball' (Waxflower)
Ficinea Fascicularis
(Flexigrass)
Tillandsia Usneoides
Calopsis Paniculata

Convallaria Majalis

Narcissus 'Paper White'
Prunus Glandulosa "Alboplena'
Dianthus 'Green Trick'
Viburnum Opulus 'Roseum'

Zantedeschia 'Green Godess'
Tulip 'Rococo'
Corylus Avellana 'Contorta'
(Contorted Hazel)
Gleichenia Polypodioides
(Coral Fern)

Calendula (Marigolds)
Genista (Broom)
Iris 'Blue Magic'
Narcissus 'Tete A Tete'
Asclepia Tuberosa
Viburnum Opulus
'Roseum'
Plagiothecium Undulatum

Asclepias Tuberosa
Liatrix Spicata
Sandersonia
Hedera Helix

Hyacinthus Orientalis 'Atlantic'
Myosotis (Forget-me-not)
Viburnum Opulus 'Roseum'
Salix Fragilis (Pussy Willow)
Gleichenia Polypodioides (Coral Fern)
Laurus Noblis (Bay Tree)
Plagiothecium Undulatum (Moss)

Chrysanthemums Spray
'Feeling Green'
Pink Pearl Pins
Midelino Canes

Hydrangea Microphylla
Seaweed

Paeony 'Sarah Bernhardt'
Papaver (Poppy)
Garlands of Mikado sticks
Placuna shells

Allium 'Purple Sensation'
Dracena Fruticosa
Hydrangea Microphylla
Papaver (Poppy)
Panicum Virgatum (Fountain Grass)

Roses 'Vendella'
Narcissus 'Paper White'
Dianthus 'Prado'
Dendrobium 'Madam Pompadour White'
Gypsophillia Paniculata 'Million Stars'
Phalaenopsis 'Kiska'
Tulip 'Tres Chic'
Aspidistra Elatior

Phalaenopsis 'Kiska'
Anthurium 'Champagne'
Dianthus 'Prado'
Tulip 'Tres Chic'
Aspidistra Elatior'Milky Way'
Mollucella Laevis
Aspidistra Elatior
Dracena Thalioides

Aspidistra Elatior
Phalaenopsis 'Okoyama'
Gypsophillia Paniculata
'Million Stars'

Nerine Bowdenii 'Ras Van Roon'
Genista (Broom)
Gerbera 'Jaska'
Roses 'Prophyta Apricot' and 'Talea'
Eucalyptus Pulverulenta

Anigozanthus Flavidus
'Bush Gold' (Kangaroo Paw)
Betula Papyrifera (Birch
branches and bark)
Phormium Tenax
Delphinium Belladonna
'Atlantis'
Eustoma Russellianum
Piccolo Pink (Lizianthus)
Cryptomeria Japonica

Liriope Muscari
(China Grass)
Hydrangea Microphylla
Roses 'Talea'
Dianthus 'Prado'
Fatsia Japonica
Paeony 'Sarah Bernhardt'

Mixed Garden Foliages
Paeony 'Sarah Bernhardt'
Roses 'Akito'
Roses Spray 'Cream Garcia'
Roses Spray 'Diadeem'
Eustoma Russellianum
'Echo Champagne'

Lilium Longiflorum
Hydrangea Microphylla
Alstromaria 'Pink
Diamond'
Syringa Vulgaris 'Ruhm
Von Horstenstein'
Syringa Vulgaris
'Madame Florent
Stepman'

Eustoma Russellianum
'Echo Geel'
Delphinium Elatum
'Alie Duyvensteyn'
Caryota Mitis (Fishtail
Palm)
Monstera Deliciosa
Xanthorrhoea Australis
(Steel Grass)

Orchids Vanda 'Pink Magic'
and 'Purple Magic'

Orchids Vanda 'Purple
Magic'
Liatrix Spicata
Midelino Canes

Asparagus Umbellatus
(Ming Fern)
Roses 'Pacific Blue' and
'Cool Water'
Eustoma 'Mariachi
Misty Blue'

Roses 'Pacific Blue'
and 'Cool Water'
Eustoma 'Mariachi
Misty Blue'
Asparagus Umbellatus
(Ming Fern)

Paeony 'Sarah Bernhardt'
Roses 'Cool Water'
Guinco sticks

Roses 'Ruby Red'
Cordyline Fruticosa
'Red Edge'

Liatrix Spicata
Roses 'Pacific Blue' and
'Blue Curiosa'
Dianthus 'Prada'
Chrysanthemum Bloom 'Green
Anastasia'
Rhapis Excelsa (Palm Leaf)

Mitsumata

Hydrangea Microphylla (Green)

Orchid Arachnis 'James Story'

Zantedeschia 'Mango'
Viburnum Opulus 'Roseum'
Hypericum 'Pinky Flair'
Frame of Mikado Sticks and
Biodegradable Netting

Orchid Arachnis 'James
Story'

Orchid Brassia 'Eternal Wind'
Midelino Canes

Zantedeschia 'Mango'
Strelitzia Reginae
Cordyline Fruticosa 'Kiwi'
Platycerum
Leucadendron 'Inca Gold'
Frame made from wood
glue, Skeleton Leaves
Sissal and Mikado Sticks

Dianthus 'Kiro'
Rose 'Illios'
Allium 'Purple Sensation'
Mitsumata

Calendula (Marigolds)
Asclepia Tuberosa
Hypericum 'Excellent Flair'
Zantedeschia 'Florex Gold'
Ornithogalum Yellow
Rhododendron
Ficinea Fascicularis
(Flexigrass)

Hydrangea Microphylla
Hedera Helix
Viburnum Tinus
Plagiothecium Undulatum (Moss)
Delphinium Elatum 'Cream Arrow'
Salix Babylonica 'Tortuosa'

Lilium 'Willeke Alberti'
Hydrangea Microphylla
Roses Spray 'Cream Gracia'
Alchemellia Mollis
Paeony 'Sarah Bernhardt'
Eustoma 'Echo Champagne'
Monstera Delisiosa
Phoenix Roebelenii

Delphinium Elatum
'Cream Arrow'
Hydrangea Microphylla
Eustoma Russellianum
'Echo Geel' and 'Echo
Champagne'
Aspidistra Elatior
Lilium 'Willeke Alberti'

Hydrangea Macrophylla
Alchemellia Mollis
Iris 'Cassablanca'

Delphinium Elatum 'Cream
Arrow' and ' Alie
Duyvensteyn'
Hydrangea Macrophylla
Delphinium Ajacis (Larkspur)
Paeony 'Sarah Bernhardt'
and 'Shirley Temple'

Lily 'Willeke Alberti'
Matthiola Incana (Stock)
Syringa Vulgaris 'Ruhm Von
Horstenstein'
Asparagus Setacues (Plumos)
Danae Racemosa (Soft
Ruscus)

Hydrangea Microphylla
Sissal Cones
Lace ribbon

Roses Spray 'Rubra'
Decorative wires and beads
Organza ribbon

Zantedeschia
'Schwarzwalder'
Pelargonium Leaf
Glitterati holder
Bullion wire trim

Dendrobium 'Madame
Pompadour'
Bullion Wire

Orchid 'Dark Pink Magic'
Decorative wires, beads
and pearls

Allium Florets
Pansy
Decorative wires

Protea Cynaroides
Pink pearl headed pins
Decorative wire

Anemone Coronaria
'Mona Lisa Blue'
Viburnum Opulus
'Roseum'
Liminium 'Emille'

Orchids Vanda 'Pink Magic'
and 'Blue Magic',
Decorative wires, beads and
pearls

Roses 'Red Prestige'
Orchid Vanda 'Red Magic'
Guinco Sticks
Bullion Wire
Wedding Belle floral foam holder

Cymbidium Orchid
'Green Glow'
Alchemellia Mollis
Danai Racemosa
Asparagus Umbellatus
Pearl detail

Zantedeschia 'Mango'
Jasminium Officianalus
Decorative wire and beads

Zantedeschia 'Mango'
Decorative wire and beads

Convallaria Majalis
Eucharis Grandiflora
Narcissus 'Paper Whites'
Gypsophillia Paniculata
'Million Stars'

Orchid Vanda 'Orange Magic'
Xanthorrhoea Australis
(Steel Grass)
Decorative Beads

Phalaenopsis 'Kiska'
Dendrobium 'Madame
Pompadour'
Decorative and
Bullion Wires
Decorative Beads
and Pearls

Rose Spray 'Diadeem'
Stephanotis Grandiflora
Aluminium Wire
Decorative wires and
beads

Roses Spray 'Diadeem'
Roses Spray 'Magenta
Diadem'
Bouvardia 'Arethusa'
Decorative Beads
Midelino Canes
Lady Heart floral foam fram

Roses 'Talea'
Roses 'Vendella'
Hedera Helix
Hypericum 'Pinky Flair'
Decorative beads, pins and
ribbon

Xanthorrhoea Australis
(Steel Grass)
Xerophyllum Tenax (Bear
Grass)
Stephanotis Grandiflora
Paeony 'Shirley Temple;
Philodendron 'Xanadu'
Danae Racemosa
Asparagus Umbellatus

Hydrangea Mirophylla
Alchemellia Mollis
Paeony 'Sarah
Bernhardt'
Paeony 'Shirley
Temple'
Bouvardia
'Bridesmaid'

Phlox Paniculata
'Bright Eyes'
Roses Spray 'Diadeem'
Roses Spray 'Cream
Gracia'
Eustoma Russellianum
'Echo Champagne'

Hypericum 'Pink Flair'
Panicum Virgatum
(Fountain Grass)
Astilbe Arendsii 'Erica'
Fatsia Japonica

Muscari (Grape Hyacinths)
Anemone Coronaria 'Mona Lisa'
Hyacinthus Orientalis 'Atlantic'
Viburnum Opulus 'Roseum'

Roses 'Red Prestige'
Roses Spray 'Macaena'
Dianthus 'Green Trick'
Skimmia Rubella
Decorative Wire Heart
Guinco Sticks

Hippeastrum 'Apple Blossom'
Nerine Bowdenii 'Ras Van
Roon'
Rose 'Talea'
Philodendron 'Xanadu'

Orchid Cymbidium
Ornithogalum Arabicum
Viburnum Opulus
Dianthus 'Prada'
Paeony 'Sarah Bernhardt'
Papaver (Poppy)
Rose Spray 'Pink Flash'
Zantedeschia 'Schwarzwalder'

Narcissus 'Soleil D'Or'
Viburnum Opulus
(Snowball Tree)
Myosotis (Forget me Nots)
Ranunculus

Plagiothecium Undulatum
(Moss)
Strawberries

Spray rose 'Mini Eden'
Limonium 'Emile'
Ranunculus
Astranta Major 'Roma'
Genista (Broom)
Myrtus Communis (Myrtle)
Rosmarinus Officinalis
(Rosemary)

Roses 'Blue Pacific'
Zantedeschia 'Pink
Glow'
Liatrix Spicata
Midelino

Dianthus 'Prado'
Roses 'Cool Water'
Paeony ' Buckeye Belle'
Papavier (Poppy)
Zantedeschia 'Schwartzwalder'
Hydrandea Microphylla

Anthurium 'Champagne'
Roses 'Silver Carema'
Roses 'Talea'
Orchid Phalaenopsis 'Kiska'
Typha Latifolia

Phalaenopsis 'Omega'
Xanthorrhoea Australis
(Steel Grass)
Roses 'Vendella'

Narcissus 'Tete a Tete' (used with bulbs)
Viburnum Tinus (Berries)
Eryngium 'Orion'
Anemone Coronaria 'Mona Lisa'
Thuya Occidentalis
Hedera Helix Arborescens (Ivy)
Plagiothecium Undulatum (flat moss)

Cornus Alba 'Sibirica' (Red Bogwood) cornus
Betula Papyrifera
Typha Latifolia
Orchid Dendrobium 'Jade Green'
Orchid Arachnis 'James Story'
Anthurium 'Choco"

Orchid Vanda 'Orange Magic'
Hedera Helix Arborescens (berried Ivy)
Ficinea Fascicularis (Flexi Grass)

Calopsis Paniculata
Helianthus 'Flame'
Roses 'African Dawn'
Hypericum 'Excellent Flair'
Leucospernum
Cordifolium Nutans (pin head Protea)

Skimmia Rubella
Anthurium 'Choco'
Myrica Gale (Bog Myrtle)
Leucadendron 'Inca Gold' and 'Safari Sunset'
Photinia 'Red Robin'
Pennisetum

Sandersonia
Typha Latifolia
Willow Canes

Abies Procera Noblis (Noble Fir)
Eucalyptus Pulverulenta
Gypsophillia Paniculata 'Million Stars'

Ornithogalum Arabicum
Rose ' Bianca'
Xanthorrhoea Australis (Steel Grass)
Decorative wire, beads and feathers

Anthurium 'Choco'
Orchid Arachnis 'James Story'
Skimmia Rubella
Hypericum 'Excellent Flair'
Aspidistra Elatior
Roses 'Red Prestige' and 'Marrakesh'
Leucospermum
Cordifolium Orange

Vanda Orchid 'Blue Magic'
Liriope Muscari (China Grass)
Detail of feathers and beads

Hippeastrum 'Red Lion' (Amaryllis)
Ficinea Fascicularis (Flexi grass)
Cranberries
Gold Aluminium wire
Decorative Stones

Orchid Arachnis 'James Story'
Aspidistra Elatior Leaves
Ilex Variegata 'Golden King'
Cetraria Islandica (Lichen Pieces)
Pots made from Betula Papyrifera (white birch bark)
Arranged onFloral Foam Cones

Mixed garden foliages
Kiwi
Pears

Anthurium 'Choco'

The 'Landscape and Seascape' photographs were shot in Barna Woods, Galway and on Barna Pier Beach, Galway. Other locations include Connemara, Co. Galway, Killarney Lakes and The Ring of Kerry; on the shores of Lough Derg, County Tipperary and beaches in Co Wexford.

Special thanks to Smithers-Oasis ® and Seamus Florist Sundries for supplying the wonderful floristry products.

ACKNOWLEDGEMENTS

Thank you to all my family and friends who have helped in so many ways.

Jo Read for the foreword and his friendship
Samantha, Louise and Patrick for wonderful help with designs and logistics
Joan and Seamus and all at 'Seamus Florist Sundries' for the studio location, help with sourcing
products and catering
John and Mike for help with designs and hospitality
Bernie, 'George Preston Florist', Newry
Shirley, Louise and Bernie for modelling
Robert and Estelle for allowing me to pick from their wonderful garden and for helping with designs
Marie Chawke and team (especially Breda) at The Aghadoe Heights, Killarney, Co. Kerry for the use of their wonderful
location for photographing my designs and for their excellent hospitality
The Very Reverend Patrick L Towers and parishioners at St Nicholas Collegiate Church,
Galway for the use of their beautiful church
The Very Reverend Dr. Stephen White and parishioners at St Flannan's Cathedral, Killaloe for allowing me to photograph in
their historic and holy Church
Stephen Short and Anthony Hart at Smithers-Oasis ® for their contribution and continued help and support
Jim Costello and team at 'Forest Produce Ltd', for the fabulous Irish foliage.
Maeve and Roy for allowing me to photograph the flowers and venue on their special wedding day
Shirley and the team at 'Branch Flowers', Galway
Gerry Harrison, 'Flower Haven'. Galway
Denise Hogan, 'Art Essence', for the wonderful hand painted glass containers
Esther Kiely for the tapestry 'love letters'
'Tolco Antiques' Galway
Graciana at 'Cakes by Desire'

Finally a big and special thanks for Annie Beagent for her styling of designs, her smiles and laughs and her great
encouragement and for all her work in editing of the book
And to David Lloyd, for his talent and professional advice. His gentle approach, his attention to detail and patience with both
myself and the Irish weather, all amalgamated to create the stunning photographs in this book

First published in 2008 by
Spirit of the Rose Ltd
71 Burford Road
Witney
Oxfordshire
OX28 6DR
www.spiritoftherose.com

Floral Designs © 2008 Richard Haslam
Photography © 2008 David Lloyd

A catalogue record for this book is available from the British Library
ISBN 978-0-9543939-5-3

Editor Annie Beagent
Photographer David Lloyd
Scanning Design and Production AB Imaging
Printed by Hill Shorter